SUPER SCIENTISTS

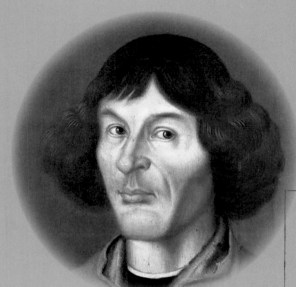

NICOLAUS COPERNICUS

Sarah Ridley

W

FRANKLIN WATTS
LONDON•SYDNEY

Franklin Watts

Published in Great Britain in 2016 by
The Watts Publishing Group

Editor in Chief: John C. Miles
Design: Jonathan Hair and Matt Lilly
Art Director: Peter Scoulding
Picture Research: Diana Morris
Original design concept: Sophie Williams

Picture credits: Blueminiu/Dreamstime: 23. The British
Library Board: 13. Endaemon/Dreamstime: 8. Forum/UIG/
Bridgeman Images: 19. Interfoto/Alamy: 18. Interfoto/
Superstock: 6. Christos Kotsiopoulos: 10-11. Museum of
Jagiellonian University: front cover cbg. Neirfy/Shutterstock:
4. Nihil Novi/CC/Wikipedia: 5. Sheila Terry/SPL: 7, 22.
Mieczyslaw Wielczko/Alamy: 12, 17. CC/Wikipedia: front
cover t & c, 1, 9, 11t, 14, 16, 20, 21.

Dewey: 520.9'2
ISBN 978 1 4451 5356 8

Printed in China

Franklin Watts
An imprint of Hachette Children's Group
Part of The Watts Publishing Group
Carmelite House, 50 Victoria Embankment
London EC4Y 0DZ

An Hachette UK Company

www.hachette.co.uk
www.franklinwatts.co.uk

FSC
www.fsc.org
MIX
Paper from
responsible sources
FSC® C104740

Contents

A merchant's son

Nicolaus Copernicus was born in 1473 into a wealthy family. His father was a merchant and the family home was often filled with visitors.

The family home in Torun, Poland.

His uncle, Lucas Watzenrode, eventually became a bishop.

19 February 1473

Copernicus is born, the youngest of four children. His name was originally spelt Niklas Koppernigk.

1480s

He starts at the local church school.

When Copernicus was only ten, his father died. His uncle, Lucas Watzenrode, looked after the family and made sure that Copernicus and his brother had a good education.

1483

His father dies.

5

To university

In 1491 Copernicus became a student in Krakow. He studied maths and natural sciences, astronomy and poetry. Much of what he learnt dated back to the time of the ancient Greeks.

Krakow, the then-capital city of Poland, as it looked in 1493.

1491-1503

When he visited Rome in 1500, Copernicus was able to observe an eclipse of the Moon.

1491–95

He attends university in Krakow with his brother.

1496

He studies Church law in Bologna.

1500

He gives a lecture on maths in Rome.

1501–03

He studies medicine at the University of Padua.

His studies continued in Italy, where he studied law and then medicine. While he was at the University of Bologna, he lived with a professor of astronomy and helped him study the night sky.

7

Hardworking star-gazer

1503

Copernicus returns to Poland and works for his uncle.

1508

He starts to form new ideas about how the Universe works.

1509

He translates ancient Greek poems from Latin and publishes them.

1510

He moves to Frombork.

Copernicus lived with his uncle in this castle at Lidzbark.

In 1503 Copernicus returned to Poland to work for his uncle, who was now a bishop. He helped with the business side of his uncle's job and also worked as his doctor.

This view of Frombork and its cathedral dates from around 1650.

Most of his spare time was spent studying the night sky and he became well known for his skill. In 1510, he moved to Frombork to help run the cathedral's business affairs.

EXPERIMENT

Like Copernicus, you can study the night sky without a telescope. Find a star map in a book or download one from the Internet (the BBC Stargazing LIVE site is very useful). It will help you find and name stars in the night sky.

The old ideas

At this time, most people believed that the Earth was at the centre of the Universe. They saw the Sun rise in the east and set in the west. People in the Catholic Church believed that God had created the world with the Earth at the centre of everything.

This photographer kept his camera in exactly the same place to make this photo showing the path of the Sun across the sky during one day.

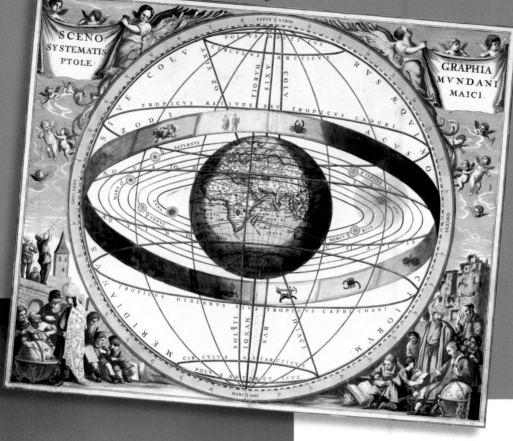

This map, made in 1660, shows Ptolemy's geocentric Universe, with the Earth at the centre.

Students learnt about the work of Greek astronomer, Ptolemy, who died in 141 CE. He placed the Earth at the centre of the Universe with the Sun and the planets revolving around it. He explained the movement of the planets across the night sky by drawing up a complicated system of loops.

11

Copernicus' new idea

Copernicus made observations of the night sky from one of the towers of Frombork Castle.

Copernicus was sure that there must be a more simple, beautiful answer to how the Universe worked. His ideas placed the Sun at the centre with the Earth and the other planets revolving around it. This was revolutionary.

BREAKTHROUGH
Copernicus worked out that the Earth and the other planets circled around the Sun. He also thought that the Earth rotated on its axis every 24 hours.

GVARDAS

PÒLO

NORTE

ORIZONTE

Libro tercero del altura del Norte.

Astronomers, and later sailors, used a cross-staff to note the height, or altitude, of stars in the night sky.

Astronomers used scientific instruments including the cross-staff, the quadrant, the triquetrum and the armillary sphere. Copernicus used them to make detailed maps of the stars and the movement of the Moon and the planets across the night sky.

1510

Copernicus writes his ideas down in a handwritten booklet.

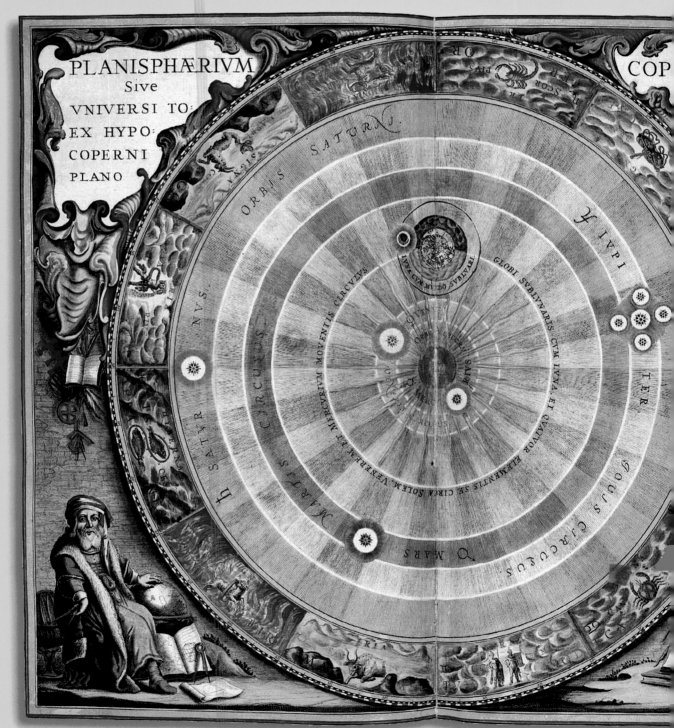

PLANISPHÆRIVM
Sive
VNIVERSI TO:
EX HYPO:
COPERNI
PLANO

COP

Copernicus worked out that the further the distance between a planet and the Sun, the longer it took for it to go around the Sun. The more he worked on the maths and his observations of the night sky, the more he was sure he was right. He let a few friends look at a written outline of his ideas.

In 1660, this illustration of Copernicus' idea, called the heliocentric model, was printed in a book of maps.

1510 onwards

Copernicus lets a few friends look at an outline of his ideas.

1512

His uncle, the bishop, dies.

1513

Copernicus has a flat area built in his garden for his scientific instruments.

BREAKTHROUGH

Copernicus worked out the correct order of the planets in orbit around the Sun.

Working for the Church

All this time, Copernicus continued to work for the Catholic Church. He helped to run Church estates, collected rents and settled arguments. He continued this work in Olsztyn when he moved there in 1516, and even organised the defence of the castle during a war.

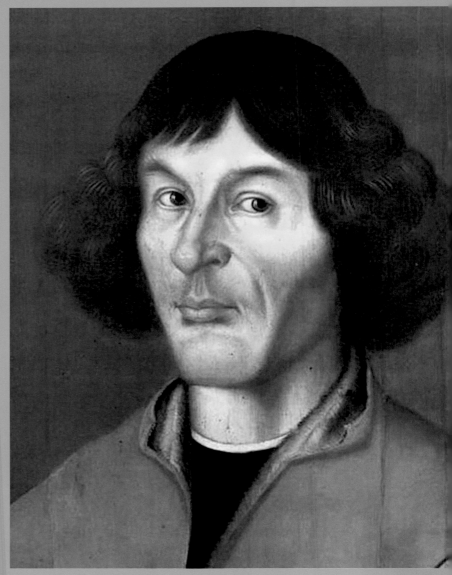

A portrait of Nicolaus Copernicus.

1513

Copernicus sends his ideas on how to make the calendar more accurate to churchmen in Rome, the centre of the Catholic Church.

1516–21

He moves to Olsztyn. He works on ideas for reforming the coinage of Poland.

Although busy with his job, he found time to draw a huge sundial on one wall of the castle where he lived. He used it to collect details of the movement of the Sun across the sky during the year, to help measure the true length of a year.

Copernicus lived in these rooms in Olsztyn Castle.

On the Revolutions

Across Europe, people are talking about Martin Luther's attacks on the Catholic Church.

1522 onwards

Copernicus returns to live in Frombork. His close friends encourage him to publish his ideas.

In this engraving, Copernicus holds a plant that shows he is a doctor.

When he was alone, Copernicus was writing down more and more calculations that proved his ideas about the Universe. This took him over twenty years but by around 1530 he had gathered everything together in a book called *On the Revolutions*.

18

Non parem Pauli gratiam requiro
Veniam Petri neq, posco, sed quam
In crucis ligno dederas latroni
Sedulus oro.

However he did not publish his book. He was afraid of what powerful people in the Church might say since most people in the Church believed that God had put Earth at the centre of the Universe. He also thought people would make fun of him.

Copernicus kept his Christian beliefs and did not want to be thrown out of the Catholic Church.

Rheticus arrives

Now in his sixties, Copernicus felt quite lonely when some of his closest friends moved away. All this changed with the arrival of a young student called Rheticus. He hoped to persuade Copernicus to publish *On the Revolutions*.

This picture shows the title page of Rheticus' book on triangles, printed in 1551.

For months, Rheticus helped Copernicus correct and prepare the book for publication. He even took the manuscript, section by section, to the best printer in Germany.

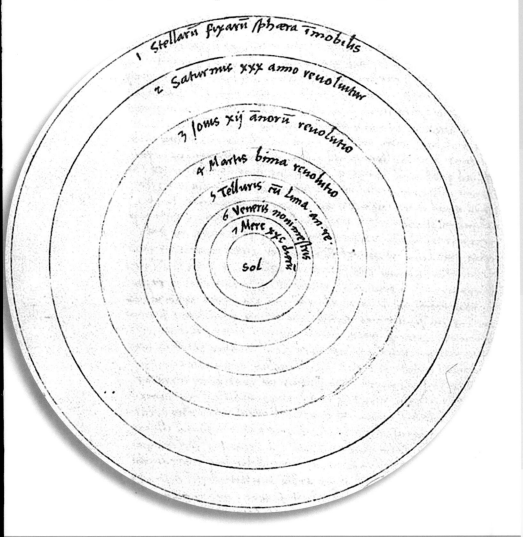

The book, On the Revolutions of the Heavenly Spheres, *contained this diagram to explain Copernicus' ideas.*

1538

Close friends leave Frombork.

1539

He is forced to make his housekeeper leave, on the orders of the bishop.

1539

Rheticus comes to stay.

1540

A short version of Copernicus' ideas is published.

Nov/Dec 1542

Copernicus has a stroke.

Death and beyond

A printed copy of *On the Revolutions of the Heavenly Spheres* reached Copernicus as he lay dying in May 1543. As Copernicus had feared, over time many people in the Church began to hate his ideas. In 1616, the Church banned his book.

It is said that Copernicus held a printed copy of his book as he died.

1543	24 May 1543	16th and 17th centuries	1616
On the Revolutions of the Heavenly Spheres is published with this longer title.	Copernicus dies and is buried in Frombork Cathedral.	His work inspires other great scientists.	The Church bans Copernicus' book – no one prints new copies.

1543 to now

In May 2010, Copernicus' bones were reburied in Frombork Cathedral with a grand funeral service.

Despite this, scientists and scholars in the 16th and 17th centuries continued to read his book. Today he is recognised as one of the world's most important scientists, who placed the Earth and the planets in their correct positions around the Sun.

1835	1945	1972	2000s	2010
The Church's ban on the book is lifted.	Nicolaus Copernicus University opens in Torun, Poland.	A crater on the Moon is named after him.	People search for Copernicus' bones under the floor of Frombork Cathedral.	Copernicus is reburied in Frombork Cathedral.

Glossary

armillary sphere A scientific instrument made up of several rings representing the position of planets and stars in the night sky, and used to measure their positions.

astronomer An expert who studies stars, planets and outer space.

axis Here, the imaginary line that passes straight through the spinning planet, Earth.

bishop A priest who has power in the Church over other priests.

coinage The coins of different values used by a country.

heliocentric The Sun (known as *helios* in Greek) at the centre, with the planets rotating around it.

Martin Luther (1483–1546) A German monk whose ideas and writings inspired a movement for change, and the formation of the Protestant Church.

merchant Someone who buys and sells things in large quantities.

natural sciences The study of biology, chemistry and physics.

observations Taking note and recording what you see.

orbit The path that a planet takes around the Sun.

quadrant A maths instrument used to measure the height of stars in the sky.

revolution One complete turn of an object that is rotating.

sphere An object shaped like a ball.

stroke A serious illness that often leaves people paralysed.

sundial An instrument used to tell the time.

triquetrum A maths instrument used to measure the position of the stars in the sky.

Universe Everything that is known to exist – our galaxy and all the others but in Copernicus' time, it meant the Sun and the planets that orbited it.

Index

Red Rock

Roca roja

Stephen Rabley

Pictures by Bob Moulder
Spanish by Rosa María Martín

BARRON'S

Lara Jones vive en Australia.

Su papá, John Jones, es actor de cine.

Su mamá trabaja para una revista de modas.

Esta noche van a ver una nueva película.

Lara no ve mucho a su padre.

"Trabajas todo el tiempo, papá", dice.

"Bueno, Lara", dice John. "Empiezo una nueva película cerca de Uluru la semana próxima. Mamá y tú pueden visitarme allí."

Lara Jones lives in Australia.

Her dad, John Jones, is a movie star.

Her mom works for a fashion magazine.

Tonight they are going to see a new film.

Lara doesn't often see her father.

"You work all the time, Dad," she says.

"OK, Lara," says John. "I'm starting a new film near Uluru next week. Mom and you can visit me there."

Dos semanas después son las vacaciones de verano.
Lara está en el aeropuerto de Sydney con su mamá.
Está muy contenta. Van a Uluru.
Pero, de repente, suena el teléfono de su mamá.
Ésta escucha dos minutos. Su cara está blanca.
"Bueno, vuelvo a la oficina ahora mismo", dice.
"Lo siento, Lara. Hay un problema *muy* grande
en la revista. No podemos ir a ver a tu papá."

Two weeks later it's the summer vacation.
Lara is at the Sydney airport with her mom.
She is very happy. They are going to Uluru.
But suddenly her mom's phone rings.
She listens for two minutes. Her face is white.
"OK, I'm coming back to the office now," she says.
"I'm sorry, Lara. There's a *very* big problem
with the magazine. We can't go to see your dad."

"Por favor, mamá", dice Lara. "Puedo ir sola."

"No. Eres demasiado joven", contesta su madre.

Mira el teléfono y entonces mira a Lara.

"Bueno, tengo una idea", dice.

"Voy a llamar a Kiku. Ella trabaja para tu papá.

Quizás *ella* pueda ir a buscarte al aeropuerto…"

"Gracias, mamá", dice Lara. "¡Qué buena idea!"

"Please, Mom," says Lara. "I can go on my own."
"No. You're too young," replies her mother.
She looks at her phone, and then she looks at Lara.
"Well, I have an idea," she says.
"I'm going to call Kiku. She works for your dad.
Maybe *she* can go to collect you at the airport…"
"Thanks, Mom," says Lara. "That's a great idea."

El avión llega tres horas más tarde. Kiku está allí.

"Hola, Lara. Soy Kiku. Mi carro está fuera."

Pronto ven una enorme roca roja en la distancia.

"Uluru", dice Lara. "¡Es preciosa!"

"Sí", dice Kiku, "y sale en la nueva película de tu padre.
Mira detrás, en el asiento."

Lara toma una carpeta blanca del asiento trasero.

Lee la primera página.

"*Roca roja*", dice, y sonríe.

The plane arrives three hours later. Kiku is there.

"Hi, Lara. I'm Kiku. My car is outside."

Soon they see a huge red rock in the distance.

"Uluru," says Lara. "It's beautiful!"

"Yes," says Kiku, "and it's in your father's new film.

Look behind you, on the seat."

Lara takes a white folder from the back seat.

She reads the first page.

"*Red Rock*," she says, and smiles.

Llegan al lugar de rodaje. Todos están muy ocupados.

Lara ve a un hombre alto con barba gris.

"Ése es Tom van Buren", dice Kiku. "Es el director."

Diez segundos más tarde Tom grita: "¡Acción!"

Hay un ruido muy grande y mucho humo.

John Jones sale en coche de un edificio.

Lara sonríe. "¿Quién hace el humo, Kiku?"

"Sam Carter", dice Kiku. "Es un hombre estupendo.

¿Lo ves? Lleva un viejo sombrero azul."

They reach the film set. Everyone is very busy.

Lara sees a tall man with a grey beard.

"That's Tom van Buren," says Kiku. "He's the director."

Ten seconds later Tom shouts, "Action!"

There's a big bang and a lot of smoke.

John Jones drives out of a building.

Lara smiles. "Who makes the smoke, Kiku?"

"Sam Carter," says Kiku. "He's a great guy.

Can you see him? He's wearing an old blue hat."

Hace mucho calor y Lara tiene sed. Ve a Sam Carter.

"Hola, soy Lara Jones", dice.

Sam sonríe. "Mucho gusto, Lara. Yo soy Sam."

"Por favor, Sam, ¿dónde hay agua?"

Sam señala. "Mira. Está allí."

A los diez minutos Lara vuelve al lugar de rodaje.

Ve a dos hombres. Ellos no la ven.

Uno dice: "El coche está listo. ¿Y la granja de Hooper?"

"Todo está bien allí también", contesta el otro hombre.

12

It's very hot and Lara is thirsty. She sees Sam Carter.

"Hello, I'm Lara Jones," she says.

Sam smiles. "Nice to meet you, Lara. I'm Sam."

"Please, Sam, where can I find some water?"

Sam points. "Look. It's over there."

Ten minutes later Lara is returning to the set.

She sees two men. They don't see her.

One says, "The car's ready. What about Hooper's Farm?"

"Everything's OK there, too," replies the other man.

Un poco más tarde, Lara ve a su padre.

"¿Te diviertes, Lara?" pregunta.

"Sí, mucho, gracias, papá", contesta Lara.

John Jones sonríe. "Bueno, ahora necesito una ducha.
Entonces tengo una reunión con el director.
Podemos comer después, tú y yo solos, ¿vale?"

"Claro, papá", dice Lara. Está muy contenta.

A moment later Lara sees her father.

"Are you having fun, Lara?" he asks.

"Yes, I am—thanks, Dad," replies Lara.

John Jones smiles. "OK, I need a shower now.
Then I have a meeting with the director.
We can have lunch after that, just you and I, OK?"

"Fine, Dad," says Lara. She is very happy.

Cuando vuelve Kiku dice: "¿Todo bien, Lara?"

"Sí, gracias", dice Lara. "¿Quieres agua?"

Es la una menos cuarto.

Todos esperan a John.

A la una y cuarto Tom van Buren dice: "¿Dónde está? Kiko, ve a buscarlo, por favor."

"Sí, señor van Buren", dice Kiku.

When she returns Kiku says, "Is everything OK, Lara?"

"Yes, thanks," says Lara. "Do you want some water?"

It's quarter to one.

Everyone is waiting for John.

At quarter past one Tom van Buren says, "Where is he?

Kiku, go and find him, please."

"Yes, Mr. van Buren," says Kiku.

Después de dos minutos, Kiku vuelve.

Tiene un papel en la mano.

"No está en su caravana", dice. Está preocupada.

Da el papel a Tom van Buren.

Lo lee en alto. *"Tenemos a John Jones.*

Queremos cinco millones de dólares.

Vamos a llamar a las seis."

Tom van Buren mira a Kiku. Está muy impresionado.

"No es posible", dice. "No puede ser verdad."

After two minutes Kiku returns.

She is holding a piece of paper in her hand.

"He's not in his trailer," she says. She is worried.

She gives the piece of paper to Tom van Buren.

He reads it aloud. *"We have John Jones.*

We want five million dollars.

We are going to call you at six o'clock."

Tom van Buren looks at Kiku. He is shocked.

"This isn't possible," he says. "It can't be true."

De repente, Lara recuerda a los dos hombres.

¡Quizás son los secuestradores!

Todos hablan a Tom van Buren.

"Tenemos que llamar a la policía", gritan.

"Perdonen", dice Lara. "Por favor, señor van Buren…"

Pero él no la oye. Lo intenta otra vez. Es imposible.

Lara tiene miedo. "Mi papá está en peligro.

Quiero ayudarle. *¿Qué puedo hacer?*"

Suddenly Lara remembers the two men.

Maybe they're the kidnappers!

Everyone is talking to Tom van Buren.

"We must call the police," they shout.

"Excuse me," says Lara. "Please, Mr. van Buren…"

But he doesn't hear her. She tries again. It's impossible.

Lara is frightened. "My dad is in danger.

I want to help him. *What can I do?*"

Lara empieza a llorar. Sam Carter la ve.

"Es terrible", dice. "Lo siento mucho."

Entonces Lara le habla de los dos hombres.

"Mi hermana vive cerca de la granja de Hooper", dice Sam.

"Está sólo a media hora de aquí."

"Tengo que ir allí ahora", dice Lara.

"No puedo esperar a la policía. ¿Puedes ayudarme?"

"Sí, claro", dice Sam. "¡Sígueme!"

Lara starts to cry. Sam Carter sees her.

"This is terrible," he says. "I'm very sorry."

Then Lara tells him about the two men.

"My sister lives near Hooper's Farm," says Sam.

"It's only half an hour from here."

"I need to go there now," says Lara.

"I can't wait for the police. Can you help me?"

"Yes, of course," says Sam. "Follow me!"

En la camioneta de Sam, Lara recuerda algo.

"¡Espera!" dice.

Rápidamente escribe una nota para Tom van Buren:

Sam y yo estamos en la granja de Hooper.

Dígaselo a la policía. Lara.

Pone la nota en el buzón de la caravana de Tom
y vuelve corriendo a la camioneta.

Sam conduce rápidamente hacia la granja de Hooper.

In Sam's truck, Lara remembers something.

"Wait!" she says.

Quickly she writes a note for Tom van Buren:

Sam and I are at Hooper's Farm.

Tell the police. Lara.

She puts the note in the letterbox of Tom's trailer
and runs back to the truck.

Sam drives fast toward Hooper's Farm.

La vieja granja está en silencio. Lara tiene miedo.

"¡Mira!" susurra. Puede ver a su padre.

Los dos secuestradores están en una habitación diferente.

"¿Qué hacemos ahora?" pregunta Lara.

"Tengo una idea", dice Sam. "¡Espera aquí!"

Después de unos minutos, vuelve

con la máquina de humo.

Pronto, la habitación se llena de humo.

Los secuestradores salen corriendo de la casa.

26

The old farmhouse is very quiet. Lara is scared.

"Look!" she whispers. She can see her father.

The two kidnappers are in a different room.

"What do we do now?" asks Lara.

"I've got an idea," says Sam. "Wait here!"

After a few minutes, he comes back
with the smoke machine.

Soon the room fills with smoke.

The kidnappers run out of the house.

En ese momento llegan dos coches de policía.

"¿Eres tú Lara Jones?" pregunta la agente de policía.

"Sí, soy yo", dice Lara. "Mi papá está en la casa.
¡Por favor, ayúdele!"

Cinco minutos después John Jones está libre.

Los policías detienen a los secuestradores
y los meten en el coche patrullero.

At that moment two police cars arrive.

"Are you Lara Jones?" asks the police officer.

"Yes, I am," says Lara. "My dad's in the house.
Please help him!"

Five minutes later John Jones is free.

The officers arrest the kidnappers
and they put them in the police car.

Un año más tarde, John gana un Óscar por *Roca roja*.

Lara, su mamá, Kiku y Sam lo están mirando.

"Éste es un día especial", dice.

"Y quiero dar las gracias a una persona muy especial.

Ven, yo soy sólo un héroe en las películas.

La heroína real aquí, esta noche, es mi hija.

¡Lara, esto es para ti!"

One year later, John wins an Oscar for *Red Rock*.

Lara, her mom, Kiku, and Sam are all watching him.

"This is a special day," he says.

"And I want to thank a very special person.

You see, I'm only a hero in the movies.

The real hero here tonight is my daughter.

Lara—this is for you!"

Quiz

You will need some paper and a pencil.

1 Here are some vehicles from the story. Copy the pictures and write the Spanish words. They are on pages 8 and 28.

el ....   dos ....

2 Match the beginnings and endings to make true sentences about the story.

1 La mamá de Lara	es director de cine.
2 El papá de Lara	trabaja para John Jones.
3 Sam Carter	es actor de cine.
4 Tom van Buren	trabaja para una revista de moda.
5 Kiku	conduce una camioneta.

3 Who says it? Find the names, then say the sentences.

1 "Trabajas todo el tiempo."

2 "Eres demasiado joven."

3 "No está en su caravana."

4 "Es terrible. Lo siento mucho."

5 "Quiero dar las gracias a una persona muy especial."

Esto es para ti.

This is for you.